COVERT NARCISSIST

7 Effective Methods Truly Used by Victims of Abuse to Cope with a Narcissist and Defend Themselves Against The Slanders and Falsehoods He Will Say About You

by Grace Richards

Disclaimer

All erudition supplied in this book is specified for educational and academic purposes only. The author is not in any way responsible for any outcomes that emerge from utilizing this book. Constructive efforts have been made to render information that is both precise and effective, but the author is not to be held answerable for the accuracy or use/misuse of this information.

Foreword

I will like to thank you for taking the very first step of trusting me and deciding to purchase/read this life-transforming book. Thanks for investing your time and resources on this product.

I can assure you of precise outcomes if you will diligently follow the specific blueprint I lay bare in the information handbook you are currently checking out. It has transformed lives, and I firmly believe it will equally change your own life too.

All the information I provided in this Do It Yourself piece is easy to absorb and practice.

Table of Contents

CHAPTER ONE

Who Are Covert Narcissists?

Covert narcissists can be described as a type of narcissist who don't fit in to the stereotypical personality that is usually associated with a narcissist. In several ways, covert narcissism may be more difficult to spot because of the narcissist's introverted character. Though it's just as dangerous as its extroverted counterpart, covert narcissism is a more hidden form of the abuse and can be trickier to pinpoint.

The main thing a covert narcissist has in common with an extroverted one is that they both use superiority to cover up their internal vulnerability. This, in turn, is also used to make their victim feel insecure or off balance about themselves or the situation. Whilst some narcissists may outright say, 'I'm better than you, so play by my rules', a covert narcissist will instead strongly hint at it - they won't be direct about it, but you'll still feel the same degradation as if they'd said it directly.

There is no 'cut and paste' set of traits for a narcissist, but some peculiar behaviors a covert narcissist can exhibit are highlighted in this chapter. Whilst they may not display all the traits or behavior outlined, a covert narcissist will exhibit some of the following throughout the course of their relationship with you. You may find that the covert narcissist in your life displays several of these traits, or you may find that they only show these behaviors from time to time. Regardless, the ways of behaving outlined here should act as a warning, at the very least, and offer you the ability to spot when you're the victim of a narcissist.

• Smugness

'None are so empty as those who are full of themselves'

Being quietly observant, judgmental and showing gestures of superiority are characteristics you'll find in a covert narcissist. They tend to do this with an air of smugness, which can leave you feeling belittled, confused and often like you're simply not good enough.

The quieter, stealthy superiority complex shows itself via aloof, detached behavior that just exudes negativity your way. Their nonverbal cues, such as sighs, eye rolls and a bored look on their face when talking to you will betray their half-hearted attempt to assure you that they're interested in what you have to say. This reassurance often feels like it's designed to make you feel even more confused because their actions are completely contradicting what they're telling you.

When you're talking or taking 'center stage' in a social setting, or even if it's just you and them, they will offer this distant and uninterested behavior. However, when they're speaking, you may find that as well as the conversation focusing on them and their views, they'll also attempt to belittle you and your opinion. Their critical, judgmental comments are, of course, very hurtful and humiliating.

This smug superiority serves as a front to mask the vulnerability the narcissist feels. This smugness can feel impenetrable, so it can be a good idea to remind yourself that their self-satisfying, superior front isn't anything to do with you.

Whist it's directed towards you, the core reason of this toxic treatment of you is down to their own insecurity and fear of being exposed as vulnerable. I'm not asking you to remind yourself of this so you can offer pity to the narcissist, but rather to help you understand that this hurtful behavior doesn't stem from anything you've said or done. The problem is theirs, not yours.

• Highly Sensitive

'Some people can't endure criticism without resentment'

Communicating with a covert narcissist is like walking on eggshells. You're worried about saying the wrong thing that may upset, offend or annoy.

Covert narcissists tend to handle criticism, or perceived criticism, very poorly. They deem negative feedback or constructive criticism a personal attack towards them. Their reaction to this isn't always graceful nor is it from a place of wanting to take that constructive criticism and use it to improve. Instead, they react in one of two ways: they either get highly defensive, and use the smug superiority described above to dismiss any unwanted feedback, or they will sulkily withdraw from the situation.

Typically, a covert narcissist won't tell you outright what is bothering them but will instead let their cold behavior towards you let you know something is up.

- **Passive Aggressiveness**

'If you're sure of yourself, you don't need to be petty or hurtful'

Passive aggressiveness in a covert narcissist can be seen via the narcissist becoming angry, hostile, and they'll often offer a fake helpfulness with no intention of ever helping you. These passive aggressive behaviors are expressed in covert ways, which are used to give the narcissist an underhanded advantage over the situation. If a covert narcissist feels threatened, they'll use passive aggressive behavior to ensure they are in control of the situation. These passive aggressive tactics are a stealthy way to exact punishment on those who dare to hurt their fragile ego.

With a covert narcissist, this passive aggression will offer a thinly disguised sense of superiority, entitlement, and is a inadvertent way to showcase their conceited view of the world. A covert narcissist is inclined to become hostile if they don't get their own way. Even if their requests or demands are unreasonable, they'll devise stealthy yet destructive ways to make you miserable for hurting their delicate sense of entitlement.

Some examples of passive aggressiveness include:

Verbal hostility: For a covert narcissist, putting other people down makes them feel self-assured and superior. Making you feel inadequate and insecure about yourself helps the narcissist relieve their own insecurities and deficiencies. This helps them seek and obtain a false sense of importance, and their critical and hostile way of speaking to you will fuel their narcissistic fire.

You may be aware of the phrase 'misery loves company', and this couldn't be truer for a covert narcissist. They will, either consciously or unconsciously, spread their misery and unhappiness to those closest to them.

In a nutshell this passive aggressive verbal hostility from the narcissist is their habitual criticism of your ideas, experiences and feelings.

Hostile humor: Very thinly veiled hostile banter or joking is often followed by the phrase 'I was just kidding' or 'can't you take a joke?' Sarcastic, hostile humor offered from a covert narcissist is their way of expressing their internal anger, rejection and/or disapproval towards you.

However, with a covert narcissist, nothing is ever upfront. Instead of outright telling you that they're feeling negatively towards you, they'll use humor as a seemingly playful way to make you feel less credible, doubtful and stupid.

The hidden intentions behind the humor are quite sinister. The narcissist uses humor as one of their many weapons to berate you covertly. When this is done in public or in front of an audience, especially when those around you laugh at the narcissist's comments, you will undoubtedly feel discredited, rejected and downright silly.

Blaming: A covert narcissist will blame others for their own failures, irresponsibility and negligence. If the narcissist fails to (or is unwilling to) follow reasonable requests, show professional conduct or even abide by social norms, this is never their fault; someone else will always get the blame.

Blaming is a form of gaslighting*, for which narcissists are renowned for. The intention behind the blameful behavior is to avoid any responsibility by manipulating the facts of the situation. A covert narcissist will distort your perception of a situation or conversation, therefore making it easier to place blame elsewhere. Often the covert narcissist will misdirect the blame onto you, thus taking the focus off the real issue at hand: their own failures and bad behavior.

It's very likely, since you're reading this book, that you're also susceptible to having blame heaped on you from the narcissist in your life.

Covert Sabotage: Covert sabotage is the narcissist's way of sneakily administering their punishment on you in a very disguised way. Examples of this could be the narcissist deliberately disclosing hurtful and harmful information, or deliberately obstructing any positive endeavors or communications. Other examples could be the narcissist deliberately undermining any agreements you've made with them. The narcissist could also purposely overspend your agreed budget, this causing you financial difficulty - but of course, you'd be the person who was handed the blame for this.

These examples are a way of summarizing the covert narcissists intentions: to punish you.

The above descriptions of passive aggressive behavior are all ways for the narcissist to manipulate and assert control over your relationship. Passive aggression can be seen in various way, not all of them so obvious. Because of this, it's important to always try to be aware of any falsehoods your partner is trying to convince you of, and to ensure that blameful behavior from the covert narcissist is met with assertive awareness of the true facts of the situation.

- **Lack of Empathy**

"One doesn't have to operate with great malice to do great harm. The absence of empathy and understanding are sufficient"

A distinct lack of empathy is a trait the covert narcissist shares with an extroverted narcissist. Both types of narcissist are so self-absorbed and self- serving that they are dismissive of other people's feelings. Often, their apparent dismissiveness of your thoughts and feelings is in fact their complete obliviousness to your feelings.

Frustratingly, even when you tell the narcissist that their behavior or attitude is upsetting you, or that it'll result in dire consequences, their response will oftenbe reverted to be about them. Your needs, wants, thoughts and feelings aren't the narcissist's main priority.

- **'I'm Special' Complex**

"Self-importance is humanity's greatest enemy"

A covert narcissist, although introverted, can still have a 'special person' complex. They may heavily hint towards being misunderstood, almost like they're so evolved nobody can understand their genius or uniqueness. This 'special person' complex can be something the covert narcissist uses as a 'woe is me' story: they may claim they feel isolated and misunderstood because they're so one-of-a-kind that nobody can possibly understand them.

Of course, this complex is just another way for the narcissist to bury his vulnerable and fearful true self.

- **Impersonal Relationships**

"Narcissists see others as impersonal objects to be manipulated for their own gain"

Covert narcissists are deeply insecure about their inability to connect with people in a meaningful way. Some of the behaviors and characteristics of a narcissist are put in place to act as a defense mechanism to keep people away or at a distance. The reason that they want to do this is to avoid being exposed for their interpersonal inadequacies and hide their incapability to forge deep relationships with others.

It can be found that some covert narcissists, due to their often-introverted nature, will focus on work or hobbies that require less human interaction, for example video games, books and films. Their jobs can often also reflect their lack of interpersonal skills, although this isn't always the case.

Whilst a covert narcissist can have friends, it's often seen that this type of narcissist doesn't form deep friendships, and they find it easier to cut people out of their life without any real regard. A covert narcissist will often have friends that they only connect with on a surface level, and anything more than that would put the narcissistic in danger of being 'exposed'.

- **Self-Absorbed**

"If you live your life as if everything is about you, you'll be left with just that: just you"

Self-centeredness and self-absorption are very common characteristics of a covert narcissist. These introverted narcissists are very poor listeners, and as such form quick opinions on people and situations.

Quiet people are widely assumed to be good listeners, although for a covert narcissist this isn't the case; the opposite is true. Because of their self-absorption, they often find things that aren't about them (or things that will directly affect them) uninteresting and unworthy of their attention.

It's ironic to think that such self-absorbed people, like the covert narcissist, also lack the self-awareness that the rest of us possess. Whilst we are fortunate to be able to have the ability to reflect on our actions and behavior, the narcissist is unable (or unwilling a lot of cases), to fully recognize just how self-absorbed they are.

Most of us are able to recognize the nuances of situations and understand that not everything can always go our way. However, covert narcissists generally only focus on their wants and, selfishly, what they deem to be agreeable. Anything else is uninteresting to them or a waste of time.

Hopefully the above explanations have helped you understand what a covert narcissist is, and now you have some idea of the behaviors and characteristics that outline this type of narcissist. Whilst this is helpful in understanding this type of abuse, actually pinpointing when you're the victim of a narcissist can be quite hard to do, especially without any guidance.

It's important to remember that the covert narcissist is possibly the hardest type of abuse to spot. Generally, they look for highly empathetic people, who will listen to their sob stories and give the narcissist the benefit of the doubt. Once the victim then begins to feel a sense of responsibility for their narcissistic partner, that's when the abuser knows that they have them reeled in and then amps up their abuse in the relationship.

The victim is then trapped in this abusive cycle. Over time, the covert narcissist will make the victim question their perception of reality, doubt themselves and make them accept blame readily. Because of this, the narcissist has ensured that they won't be held accountable for their behavior by the victim.

As with all narcissists, covert narcissists do have a predictable pattern of behavior when it comes to romantic partners. In the beginning, they may appear to idealize their partner. This acts as bait for the victim. Once the victim is hooked in, the narcissist will then devalue their partner, and (as you sadly may be all too aware), this then causes the victim to chase the love and adoration they received from their abuser previously.

The victim is unaware that this devaluation from the abuser is done with sinister and purposeful intent. After this, the narcissist will then discard their partner.

The covert narcissist may appear as a calm, quiet and polite person to most people. However, when you're in a relationship with one, they're often cold, distant abusive and demeaning. Jekyll and Hyde can be a good way of describing their personality and treatment of you.

Often, a covert narcissist is seemingly quiet and can usually be described as being meek and inoffensive by most people, but behind closed doors it can be a very different story. They thrive of their partners failures and upset. It's not an uncommon game for a covert narcissist to set you up for failure or upset. The crazy-making thing about this is that the narcissist will then punish you for the aforementioned failure. Introverted narcissists are also renowned for making empty promises, without ever having any intention of delivering. They will then get a twisted kick out of your reaction when they fail to deliver, often making themselves appear as the victim, and making you look unreasonable and selfish with unbearable expectations.

A hurtful and frustrating aspect to this behavior of making promises without delivering is when the narcissist will deny ever making that promise in the first place. This gaslighting behavior can often make you think you're losing your mind, and make you question your perception of reality. This is known as 'percepticide*'.

The best way to describe a covert narcissists internal feelings would be 'conflicted'. Whilst the narcissist wants to be worshipped and adored, and they do think quite a lot about themselves, they are also incredibly insecure about themselves. This internal conflict creates the unbalanced, manipulative and willful confidence-sucker that is the covert narcissist.

CHAPTER TWO

How To Recognize A Covert Narcissist

Covert narcissists are the most cunning, conniving and difficult personalities to detect. They are gifted chameleons who are socially skilled and capable of expressing a convincing pseudo empathy. Most people are fooled and disarmed by the covert narcissist.

Examples of how they operate include:

1. Covert narcissists use secrecy and stealth to control your emotions and weaken you emotionally and psychologically.

2. Covert narcissists demean and humiliate you when you are the most vulnerable.

3. Covert narcissists convince others they are good people who can be trusted and are worthy of your respect.

4. The covert is obsessed with ultimate control over others, especially those closest to him or her.

5. Covert narcissists constantly plot and plan how to manipulate and exploit their competitors.

Learn how to recognize the covert narcissist by studying his hidden traits, baits and snares. They play the "good person" or the "martyr" roles to the hilt. They are like fine method actors. If you don't recognize them at first, don't blame yourself. They are so clever and smooth with their psychological camouflage they are very difficult to detect.

Pay close attention to the intuitive cues that you are receiving and don't wave them off as irrational or insignificant. Embrace these insights.

Develop a regular practice of psychological, emotional and mental grounding. This includes a form of meditation, prayer, affirmations, quiet times with Nature and other forms of activity that are calming and restorative. Part of this practice is instilling a sense of firm respect for your personal psychological boundaries. As you move through each day, develop a deep appreciation for your unique authentic original self.

An essential part of the healing and restorative process is in activating the parasympathetic nervous system. Here we recover, retreat into peace and calmness and restore our sense of security and psychological grounding. One of the finest ways to move into the parasympathetic is through acupuncture. This ancient Chinese medical practice the patient is treated to balance all of the systems of the body including the calming and balancing of the nervous system. So often if you have lived with and put up with the abuse of a narcissistic personality, you body and mind are in a state of fight or flight mode. Acupuncture is a powerful method for helping the patient to shift into the rest, repose and restorative mode.

Another pathway to the parasympathetic is through engrossing ourselves in beauty in all of its miraculous forms. Whether it is Nature and our immersion in its beauty and mystery or finding an art form that we love, the experience of beauty puts us into the center of the parasympathetic nervous system. Here we feel at home and secure.

You are on the road to life healing. Always remember and value who you are as a unique individual. Pay close attention to your intuition: our protector, guide and the deep source of perpetual inspiration and creativity.

Understanding that you are dealing with a covert narcissist is the first step in knowing how to interact with them. As previously said, it is not always easy to recognize it, but at least 5 common characteristics can be identified that unmask it in our eyes:

1. Constant pursuit of unobtrusive admiration

Unlike overt narcissistic disorder, coverts don't want to be the center of attention overtly . All this is explained by their shy and reserved air with which interpersonal relationships begin, especially those of love. This means that the search for admiration for them does not happen with blatant gestures or as the leader of a group: they expect it for their way of being , for those fantasies of fame and glory that harbor unbeknownst to everyone.

The reserved and shy attitude changes significantly when the spotlight is not on them as they hoped. This is how they unleash one of their most dangerous weapons, namely passive-aggressive behaviorNarcissists will never reveal their anger or frustration by making dialogue impossible due to the treatment of silence they reserve for their "victims".

2. Shyness and vulnerability

In everyone's imagination, a narcissistic behavior is what he sees of delusions of protagonism and grandiosity , as well as fantasies of success and fame. This attitude is explained by the exhibitionistic need of narcissistic subjects to be recognized by others. This is one of the significant characteristics that most covert narcissists lack and that can deceive people who come into contact with them, first of all partners.

It is not infrequently heard that many women are fascinated not by Nietszche's "superman", but by the shy and solitary boy , who opens up "alone" with them, telling about his difficult life. However, it is good to know that exhibiting pain is never a good thing. As with other disorders, covert narcissists use the air of a victim in a relationship to get everything they want from those around them. The sense of narcissistic superiority and the drive for grandiosity have not, therefore, disappeared, but only take on a different facade , the timid, modest or vulnerable one.

The strength of this narcissist is no longer his talents, as for the overts, but his bad luck or his defects , because of which he believes he is entitled to a special treatment from the more fortunate and happier others.

3. Only apparent empathy

If that of an overt narcissist is an always ascertained lack of empathy, that of a covert personality could be defined as more " devious ". In fact, the empathy he demonstrates is one-way, that is, only for himself . To do this, he shows himself on many occasions as a victim, perhaps blaming others for the mistakes he made or for any other reason. By playing the card of victimhood he often manages to confuse those around him of his lack of empathy towards others.

Also, when narcissists hurt someone with their attitude and point it out, they completely cut off communication and prove disinterested.. It is precisely from such behavior that the importance they give only to themselves is highlighted, being unable to have genuine feelings for others.

4. Difficulty in interpersonal relationships

Another typical trait of the covert narcissist is that of " social withdrawal ". This happens because if on the one hand an overt subject proves to be brilliant, enterprising and breezy towards everyone, the covert personalities are much more selective in terms of attendance . All of this fits perfectly with their shy and reserved facade with which they introduce themselves at the beginning of a relationship.

Lack of close friends or acquaintances is a sign that you need to pay close attention to: People with covert narcissism choose people to surround themselves with solely based on their own advantage . He is opportunistic and calculating , especially when it comes to economic profit.

Removed from their inner circle of "friends," covert narcissists will not know how to relate to others and will not even try. They ignore all those who do not respect that image and selection criteria to become part of their knowledge, looking at them with an air of superiority .

5. Devaluation of the partner

Being struggling with a narcissistic partner is never easy, quite the opposite. Depending on the type of narcissism with which one has to confront, one experiences attitudes that strongly damage self-esteem . The first of all is that of devaluation . If a narcissist feels that he is too dependent on his partner, he tries to restore order - that is, power - within the couple by undermining his self-confidence and devaluing it. Furthermore, since the covert subject has serious self-esteem deficiencies , he tends to look for a partner who makes him "shine" in the eyes of others, only for his sole need for superiority .

On the other hand, however, if the partner obtains better results than hers, especially in the workplace and / or economic, she will feel a strong envy towards her, which will show itself, precisely, with an attack aimed at her self-confidence. Therefore, we understand how a relationship like this is toxic and dangerous , even in the short term.

Narcissists don't like themselves. Deep down, narcissists feel the space in between the façade they show the world and their shame-based self. To fill this gap narcissists use harmful defense systems that destroy relationships and trigger pain and damage to their enjoyed ones.

Abuse is abuse, no matter what the abuser's medical diagnosis. If you're a victim of abuse, the primary difficulties for you are:

- Clearly identifying it.

- Developing an assistance system.

- Knowing how to strengthen and safeguard yourself.

Blanket declarations and generalizations.

Deadly narcissists aren't always intellectual masterminds-- a number of them are intellectually lazy. Rather than making an effort to think about various viewpoints carefully, they generalize anything and everything you state, making blanket declarations that don't acknowledge the subtleties in your argument or consider the numerous perspectives you have regarded.

On a bigger scale, generalizations and blanket declarations invalidate experiences that do not fit in the schemas, unsupported assumptions and stereotypes of society; they are likewise used to preserve the status quo. While those do happen, they are uncommon, and in this case, the actions of one become identified the behavior of the majority while the particular report itself remains unaddressed.

These daily microaggressions likewise take place in harmful relationships. If you raise to an egotistical abuser that their behavior is undesirable for instance, they will frequently make blanket generalizations about your hypersensitivity or generalize such as, "You are never ever satisfied," or "You're constantly too delicate" instead of attending to the real problems at hand. You may be oversensitive at times, but it is also possible that the abuser is cruel and likewise insensitive the bulk of the time.

Keep your reality and resist generalizing statements by understanding that they remain in truth kinds of black and white illogical thinking. Hazardous people wielding blanket declarations do not represent the full richness of experience.

5. Deliberately making misrepresentation of your thoughts and feelings to the point of absurdity.

In the hands of a deadly narcissist or sociopath, your differing viewpoints, experiences and genuine feelings get seen as character flaws and evidence of your irrationality.

Narcissists weave tall stories to reframe what you're really saying as a way to make your viewpoints look abhorrent or ridiculous. Let's state you raise the reality that you're dissatisfied with the way a toxic pal is talking to you. In action, she or he may put words in your mouth, stating, "Oh, so now you're best?" or "So I am a bad individual, huh?" when you have done nothing but express your feelings. This allows them to revoke your right to have thoughts and emotions about their improper habits and instills in you a sense of regret when you try to develop limits.

This is also a popular type of diversion and cognitive distortion that is known as "mind-reading." Poisonous people often presume they understand what you're thinking and feeling. They chronically leap to conclusions based on their own triggers rather than going back to evaluate the scenario mindfully. They act accordingly based upon their own misconceptions and fallacies and make no apologies for the harm they cause as a result. Well-known for putting words in your mouth, they illustrate you as having an intent or outlandish perspective you didn't possess. They accuse you of thinking about them as hazardous-- even before you've got the opportunity to call them out on their behavior-- and this also functions as a kind of preemptive defense.

Simply stating, "I never ever said that," and leaving should the individual continue to implicate you of doing or starting something you didn't can assist to set a firm limit in this type of interaction. Long as the hazardous individual can digress and blameshift from their own habits, they have succeeded in persuading you that you need to be "shamed" for giving them any sort of sensible feedback.

Altering the subject to evade responsibility.

It is a literal variation from the real subject that works to redirect attention to various problems completely. Narcissists do not want you to be on the subject of holding them accountable for anything, so they will reroute conversations to benefit them. This type of diversion has no limitations in terms of time or subject content and typically starts with something like "What about the moment when"

On a different level, these diversions work to derail conversations that challenge the status quo. A discussion about gay rights, for instance, might be thwarted quickly by somebody who generates another social justice concern simply to sidetrack individuals from the primary argument.

Don't be thwarted-- if somebody pulls a switcheroo on you, you can exercise what I call the "damaged record" approach and continue specifying the truths without giving in to their distractions.

Covert and obvious risks.

Narcissistic abusers and otherwise harmful people feel threatened when their excessive sense of privilege, a grandiose sense of self and a false sense of superiority are challenged in any way. They are prone to making unreasonable needs on others-- while punishing you for not living up to their difficult to reach expectations.

Instead of taking on disagreements or compromises maturely, they set out to divert you from your right to have your own identity and point of view by trying to instill fear in you about the repercussions of disagreeing or complying with their needs. To them, any difficulty results in an ultimatum and "do this or I'll do that" becomes their daily mantra.

If somebody's response to you setting borders or having a varying viewpoint from yours is to threaten you into submission, whether it's a very finely veiled hazard or an obvious admission of what they intend to do, this is a red flag of someone who has a high degree of privilege and has no strategies of compromising. Take hazards seriously and show the narcissist you imply organization; report them whenever legally feasible and possible.

Name-calling.

Narcissists often blow anything they perceive as a danger to their superiority out of percentage. In their view, only they can ever be ideal and anyone who dares to say otherwise develops a narcissistic injury that leads to egotistical rage.

The most affordable of the low turn to narcissistic rage in the form of name-calling when they can't think about a better method to control your viewpoint or micromanage your emotions. Name-calling is a quick and easy method to degrade you, put you down, and insult your intelligence, behavior or appearance while invalidating your right to be a different individual with a right to his or her perspective.

Name-calling can also be used to slam your insights, beliefs, and viewpoints. A well-researched viewpoint or notified opinion all of a sudden become "ridiculous" in the hands of a covert narcissist who feels threatened by it and can not make a respectful, persuading counterclaim. Instead of targeting your argument, they target you as an individual and look to undermine your reliability and intelligence in any way they possibly can. It's essential to end any interaction that includes name-calling and communicates that you won't endure it. Don't internalize it: recognize that they are turning to name-calling since they are deficient in higher-level approaches.

CHAPTER THREE

Manipulation

We may have an uneasy kind of sensation in our gut that doesn't match the manipulator's words or really feel coerced into agreeing with a request. Most individuals react in ways which aggravate abuse or play into the hands of the abuser as well as feel guilty, but retreat and allow inappropriate behaviours. If you had a manipulative father and mother, it may be more difficult to identify in a companion, because it's familiar.

The ancient wisdom to "recognize your enemy" is necessary when you are dealing with a manipulator. Being able to find these concealed arrows enables you to respond strategically to covert manipulation. Having a good understanding of what they are up to will empower you.

Whenpeople behave passive-aggressively, what appears passive or defensive is concealed aggression. It's open to question to what extent their actions is conscious or unconscious.

To the victim, it matters not. The effect is very much the same. Being overly-empathetic puts you at risk of being maltreated over and over. When someone assaults you overtly or secretly, they're being hostile. These manipulators deliberately say and do things to obtain what they want for power as well as control.

For people with logically disturbedcharacter, such as narcissists and some individuals with borderline personality challeges, their tactics are not unconscious in such a way that defensemechanism usually operate. However, their actions is so habitual that with time it ends up being reflexive. They do not think about it ordinarily, but are still aware of it.

Goals of a Manipulator

The objective or goal of all forms of manipulation is to get influence necessary to meet our needs but regular manipulators do so for power as well as control and make use of deceptive and violent techniques. Manipulators maintain supremacy via continual, persisting, emotional control, abuse, as well as forceful control. Commonly they're passive-aggressive. They might lie to be caring or pretend to be stunned by your complaints all to deflect any criticism and to continuously behave in an undesirable fashion. In maintaining control to achieve what they desire, manipulators usually aim:

1. To stay clear of being confronted.

2. To make you doubt yourself as well as your assumptions

3. To place you on the defensive

4. To stay clear responsibility

5. To conceal their hostile intent

6. To not have to change

Eventually, you get victimized as you can lose confidence in yourself and your perceptions as well as feelings. Gaslighting is a treacherous, disabling kind of control.

Covert Manipulative Tactics

Manipulation can include obvious aggression, such as narcissistic abuse, criticism, as well as subtle types of emotional abuse. Commoncovert weapons of manipulators include: complaining, guilt, lying, comparing, denying, feigning innocence or lack of knowledge (e.g." Who? me !?"), blame, bribery, threatening, mind games, presumptions, "foot-in-the-door," reversals, emotional blackmail, evasiveness, neglecting, inattention, fake issue, compassion, apologies, flattery, as well as favours and gifts.

Common tactics are described below:

• Lying

Regular liars occasionally lie when it's unnecessary. They aren't lying due to the fact that they're scared or guilty, but to confuse you and do what they desire. Some at the same time put you on the defensive with allegations and other manipulative tactics. Lying may additionally be indirect through uncertainty and/or omission of material information though everything else claimed is true. For instance, a cheater may state he or she was working late or at the fitness center, but not admit to a cheating rendezvous.

- **Denial**

This isn't an unconscious denial, like not recognizing you've being abused, have a dependency, or are staying clear of facing challenging realities. This is mindful denial to disclaim knowledge of promises, agreements, and behavior. The denial also includes reduction and justification or excuses. The manipulator mostly acts as ifyou are only making a big deal over nothing or rationalizes and excuses his or her actions to make you question on yourself or to get your compassion.

- **Avoidance**

Manipulators like to avoid being confronted and taking responsibility in any way possible. They may avoid conversations concerning their habits by simply refusing to discuss it. This could be combined with accusations, like, "You're always troubling me," putting you on the defensive with shame, guilt or blame.

When a manipulator changes the subject, avoidance can be undetectable and subtle. It may be concealed with boasting, praises, or remarks you want to listen to, like, "You know exactly how much I appreciate you." You could fail to remember why you were upset to begin with.

One more avoidance method is evasiveness that obscures the facts, perplexes you and plants uncertainty. When you're hopeful regarding a relationship, it's simple to give someone the benefit of doubt and go into denial yourself. Trust them when you have doubts!

- **Blame, Guilt, and Shame**

These strategies involve projection, a form of defence where the manipulator accuses others of his or own actions. Manipulators believe "The ideal defence is a good offense." By changing the blame, the aggrieved person is now on the defensive. The manipulator continues to be innocent as well as complimentary to continue, while their victims feel regret and shame.

Manipulators criticize their sufferers or any person else. Watch out for an apology that is really another manipulation. Addicts commonly blame their dependency on various other people, their very demanding boss or "bitchy" partner. A criminal accused without any defense will attack the police or their techniques of collecting evidence. Rapists used to be able to strike the reputation of their sufferers.

Guilt-tripping as well as shaming somehow shifts the focus onto you, which compromises you while the abuser feels exceptional. Martyrs use guilt when they imply or say, "After all I've done for you ..." sometimes mixed with criticism that you're unappreciative or egocentric.

Shame goes past guilt to make you feel less adequate or inadequate. It's demeans you as a person, your traits, or purpose, not just your actions. "The children would really behave if they had a father that understood how to effectively parent (or, made a good living.)" Making comparism is a subtle, but effective form of shaming. It's harmful when parents compare brother or sisters with each other or with friends. Some partners compare their lover to their ex-spouse to have the top hand by making their companion feel inferior.

Guilt and shaming might consist of "criticizing the victim." You find evidence on your partner's phone that he or she is flirting. Your companion acts annoyed that you went right into the phone. Now he or she has changed the emphasis onto you. By blaming you, your companion has prevented a confrontation about flirting, and may also lie regarding it, minimize, or circumvent it completely. You, the actual victim, feel guilty for snooping, destroying any kind of warranted rage, and might consequently enable the flirting to continue unaddressed.

- **Intimidation**

Intimidation isn't always with straight threats, but can be subtle. It can be accomplished with an appearance or tone and statements like: "I constantly get my way;" "No one's irreplaceable." "The grass isn't any greener;" "I have good friends in high places;" "You're not so young any longer;" or "Have you taken into consideration the repercussions of that decision?" Another approach is telling a story meant to provoke fear, such as: "She left her hubby and lost her kids, their house, whatever."

Playing the Victim

This is quite different from blaming the victim. Rather than blame you, this "poor me" tactic arouses your regret and sympathy so you'll do their bidding. "I don't know what I'll do if you don't help me." If you leave, a lot more disordered people will threaten suicide. It can also take the form of, "You do not care about me;" "Nobody helps me" "Why do you treat me like this?"

Your compliance brings abouanimosity, harms the relationship, and allows contuousmanipulation. Guilt over somebody else's behavior or circumstance is unreasonable guilt.

Theabove tactics are quite destructive. You can forgive, but don't forget. Manipulation is likely to continue. With time, this is traumatic and can drastically damage your self-worth. Being aware is the very first step. You might require assistance to see things clearly. Draw up discussions and also try to identify all the tactics used. Better still is not taking the words of the manipulator personally and discovering ways to react.

Affective Manipulation

Narcissistic manipulation is a type of mental dependency, where the narcissist requires continuous significance, validation, "special treatment,", or appeasement to enable him or her feel good about him or herself. This attitude of craving to be "put on a pedestal" explains to a large extent, the narcissist's sense of entitlement, conceit, and self-absorption.

Have you ever came across a narcissist before? Been a victim of one? Have you been lucky not to have ever needed to relate with a narcissist at any period in your life? Narcissists are language masters who use words to trick, seduce, mislead, and coerce. Spoken hoax is their favored technique of control and they have a talent for stating the best thing at the correct time to confuse, belittle and degrade the other individual.

They redicle their victims, purposefully seeking to make them feel useless so that they might subjugate them to their will. The unrelenting mind video games of the narcissist are exceptionally damaging to those on the receiving end; they can result in anxiety, depression, and a whole host of other mental results.

Victims are left distressed by the barrage, with psychological discomfort that appears to have no end. They end up being psychologically maimed by the assault, not knowing what is taking place or how to escape from it.

Knowledge of their ways will assist you in forming a shield against their attacks and prepare you for a fast escape if you ever get drawn in by one. Even if you have already suffered abuse at the hands of a narcissist, a better understanding of how they operate might be of help in the process of your recovery. It might help to encourage you that you were a victim and not merely a participant in the entire episode. Irrespective of the role you think you played, it is most likely that you were just doing the narcissist's will.

Below are just some of the significant ways in which a narcissist will exploit language to effectively manipulate his (or her) victim:

• Low-level Stealth Abuse

This is an umbrella for the practically ceaseless stream of small, nearly insignificant comments that form the foundation of a narcissist's spoken abuse.

This is how they will generally begin to apply control over their victims, starting early on in the relationship when it might appear nothing more than a small defect in their otherwise charming behavior.

Frequently with a friendly smile on their face, they will state things like "you're an extremely delicate thing aren't you?" or "no, you have actually misconstrued what I was saying." These are the starts of a lot longer procedure to wear the victim down, but they are seldom seen for what they are because of their appearing insignificance.

This sort of surprise abuse will continue throughout a relationship as an accompaniment to more insidious attacks.

- **The "Special Relationship" Myth**

Another thing that narcissists will do, particularly at the beginnings of a relationship, is to persuade their victim of the unique and unique bond they have. They may use expressions such as "I've never felt this kind of love for anybody before" or "The feelings I have for you is so much more than what many people believe love is."

This is a type of grooming that starts to plant the seeds for the victim's future tolerance of more painful abuse. They are misguided into thinking that all the very best relationships are explosive and passionate and that this is an indication that theirs is something very precious. The victim ends up being convinced of this "reality" and, therefore, finds it tougher to escape with every passing day.

• I Didn't Mean It/ I Was Only Joking

Another manner in which a narcissist will inflict their spitefulness on their victims is to continuously dismiss insults or criticisms by declaring that they didn't actually mean them.

They know full well that the preliminary remark will have injured their victim, but, make their excuses to conceal their harmful intent. They say they were joking, but, in the actual sense, they were craftily going on the offensive to maneuver themselves into a dominant position.

This sort of language further conditions the victim to accept the narcissist's behavior. It puzzles them and makes them uncertaing regarding whether they ought to be offended. When to view a remark as an insult and when to take it as a joke merely hands power over to the narcissist to say what he likes, not knowing.

Mind Games Which Can Be Used By Narcissists For Manipulation

There is a saying that you can only love others if you love yourself. This is certainly true in many situations, being at peace with yourself makes it much easier to have a healthy relationship . But self-love can also become independent. Then it turns into narcissism.

The dangerous thing about a relationship with a narcissist is manipulation.Your partner can wrap you around their finger and suddenly lets you do things that you don't recognize yourself? Watch out.

Because even those who think they have a good knowledge of human nature can fall victim to a narcissist - because they play so skillfully with our feelings that we rarely notice.

Mind games of a narcissist

• He uses his importance as an excuse

It's all about him. But a narcissist would never tell you that. Rather, he packs his self-love in a victim role and uses it consistently. How does it look in everyday life? Here are a few examples: He would love to come to dinner with your family - but without him the project at work will never be finished. The boss asked about him explicitly - even though he would much rather be with you. His friend urgently needs his help - only he can stand by him in the situation.This way, a narcissist always puts their needs first, but manipulates you so much that you don't even realize it . Rather, he gives you the feeling that he is the good one, but the world just needs him more than you.

- **He makes fun of your feelings**

That often gives you the feeling that you are wrong. Strictly speaking, he can't even do something about it: Narcissists have difficulty putting themselves in other people's shoes. For many people, empathy is a foreign word.As a result, they simply don't understand many problems - humor is one way of dealing with them. He hurts your feelings so much that you suddenly question them yourself.

- **A narcissist makes you feel like you are flawed**

Let's not get one another wrong: Everyone has faults and that's a good thing. But it's not the best way to rub it under someone's nose again and again - especially your partner.

By the way, with this game he manipulates you and himself twice. Often times, a narcissist will consciously pick your flaws and use them against you when you are vulnerable. You feel uncomfortable and, absurdly, still look up at him even more. Because often a narcissistic partner holds up against you your weaknesses compared to his strengths. At the same time, he manipulates himself. Narcissists are arrogant and self-confident. But this self-love is often just a way to hide your insecurity. So he feels better when you're uncomfortable. This paradox does not belong in any relationship - and yet it is one of the most popular mind games of a narcissist.

How you can recognize manipulation by a Narcissist

Breaking up with narcissists can be very difficult. If they are not done with you yet, then they will beg you to stay. And if you feel dependent on them , then begging and making false promises will also be effective.

It takes a lot of strength to break away from a narcissist because these people are so good at lying. They have been lying all their lives, they lie to themselves and to others. Your ego is inflated to cover up your inferiority complexes. But it's all just a delusion.

Narcissists know exactly what stories to tell you in order for you to stick with them out of pity or shame. They are so good at lying that their victims feel like they are insane themselves.

So they are very good at justifying their bad behavior.

Some will say: "I can't help it, I'm so damaged, I have to drink alcohol or sniff coke or whatever," "That's why I'm acting so badly, so please understand and forgive me. Therefore, in their eyes, you have to excuse both - the abuse of drugs and the emotional abuse of yourself.

The point behind it: Narcissists want you to feel guilty for questioning their motives in the first place. If Neo's clients addressed that their narcissistic partner was aggressive, insensitive, or behaved inappropriately, then a defense would have come immediately.

Make your favorite phrase "I know I'm better" so that victims think the problems are in the past (addictions or a difficult ex-partner).

Narcissists follow a simple pattern

"For example, they say, I was addicted to sex," Neo said. "Or: I was addicted to sex, but I'm much better. And whenever they make a mistake, they will say that they couldn't help it and relapsed. "

They will keep talking about their past and the difficult life they had. You will hardly meet a narcissist who does not claim to have grown up in difficult circumstances.

"They will say that they are only this way because of their past or because their mother hurt them. Or it's her father's fault, "said Neo. Narcissists also get angry when you don't appreciate the seemingly small things that they have accomplished. They want praise from you for their "normal" behavior, and they will offend you if you don't keep congratulating them.

They'll remind you of the one week when they drank less. And that you are ungrateful. That you didn't see that they wanted to improve. The changes are extremely small, but narcissists will inflate them because every little good deed is the greatest in their eyes. That is their currency.

Some narcissists blame their friends for their behavior and the environment in which they live. Others say again that their partner is to blame for inciting them.

In the early stages of a relationship, narcissists overwhelm their victim with attention and affection, to be the greatest person. When you are sure that you have your partner on the line, you show the real you.

Your lies have no limits

Narcissists will sometimes poke the pity card and tell you about their emotional problems. And then they will use it against you because you are bad people if you don't accept these problems as an excuse.

"They will say that they are addicted to alcohol or drugs because they are depressed or have anxiety disorders," Neo said. "My ex-boyfriend told me about his alleged borderline illness. Borderliners cannot control their emotions. And that is the reason why he is paranoid and does not want me to talk to other people. "

There are very dysfunctional narcissists who even pretend to be sick to get what they want. For example, one of Neo's clients bought her ex-husband a house because she thought he had serious cancer.

Narcissists get better and better at manipulating others as they learn more and more tricks. That's why they get away with all the delusion.

The only thing you can do: avoid these people. Break up - as soon as you can as soon as you realize that they have no empathy.

CHAPTER FOUR

What triggers a narcissist behavior?

The effects of narcissistic traits are the most pronounced when examining interpersonal relationships. Initially, individuals with a high number of narcissistic traits are able to behave in ways that are amicable to others, however over time these relationships deteriorate, especially as they become more intimate, trait comes to be more apparent—for instance by causing distress to significant others .

Therefore, to understand the mechanisms behind their behavior it would be advantageous to examine narcissistic individuals in ongoing social interactions with others.

Historically, behavioral economists have used paradigms whereby they can examine individuals as they are faced with the opportunity to retaliate or reciprocate in ongoing social interactions. Their results highlight two key aspects of social behavior: first, people tend to be more generous when faced with the possibility of punishment, so they behave more strategically.

Second, individuals tend to punish others that they deem unfair. The latter could be because individuals want to enforce social norms or because they are retaliating out of feelings of anger. Thus, the use of economic paradigms to investigate individual differences in relation to personality traits, especially those who have problems with interpersonal relationships, could be a viable empirical tool to help understand the mechanisms underlying narcissist behavior.

Narcissistic social behavior has primarily been investigated from the active position—thereby putting the narcissistic individual in a role where they are the first movers and not reacting to another's actions.. In line with common narcissistic traits, which indicate a tendency to be interpersonally exploitative and self-absorbed, the results generally demonstrate that narcissistic individuals behave more selfishly and less prosocially.

However examining how narcissists behave when they are in the reactive, or respondent role, has yet to be investigated.

Parenting errors as the most important causes of narcissistic personality disorder

Psychologists agree that pathological narcissism has its origins in early childhood and in relationships with parents, especially the mother. Research has shown that genetic factors also play an important role in the development of this mental disorder. However, hereditary predisposition can never be defined as the sole cause of the disorder.

Family relationships are crucial for the healthy psychological development of a child in the first few years of life. People who suffer from narcissistic personality disorder have experienced exposure from their parents in early childhood, which has led to limited or negatively impaired development of individuality and self-esteem. As a result, the affected children either had to suppress certain needs or were able to live them out in an uninhibited manner, since parental upbringing set no limits. As a result, as adults they have not learned the ability to intuitively understand their own needs and feelings and to show or enforce them appropriately in a situation.

Neglect and Parental Distance as Causes of Narcissistic Behaviours.

Most people who suffer from this disorder did not receive enough attention or recognition from their mother in their early childhood. The first months of life in particular are formative in this context, because every baby has the natural need to be unconditionally loved by its mother and to feel her physical closeness incessantly. If this basic need is not met or if it is linked to certain requirements, the child begins to orientate itself to the expectations of the caregiver, which leads to a separation and suppression of their own feelings.

In further development, constant confirmation from the outside world must increasingly replace the lack of attention from the mother or another caregiver. Children who are constantly criticized or disciplined by their parents are also exposed to an increased risk of developing narcissistic disorders later in life, since they are not given the opportunity to develop according to their own dispositions and to experience them positively.

An overprotected childhood as a trigger for pathological narcissism

The disturbed self-image that results from parental rejection or neglect is contrasted with such that develops from pampering and exaggerated admiration in childhood and can also trigger a narcissistic personality disorder. Many people who suffer from this condition grow up with an over-dominant single mother or in a problematic parenting relationship in which one parent overstrains them. Children who constantly experience excessive affection and love from their parents and who are consistently kept away from any problematic situations are also confronted with limitations in normal development.

If admiration and preference become life-determining factors, children do not learn to endure defeats in everyday life, at school or in interpersonal relationships. They develop into adults who cannot see problems as challenges, but are completely helpless when they are asked to find solutions and compromise. The role as the most important figure in the life of the parents often means that the child cannot reflect his behavior, does not experience any social resonance and also does not learn to behave respectfully and appropriately for a situation. Consequently, as an adult, they cannot develop any respect for other people and constantly feel superior in their social dealings.

CHAPTER FIVE

How To Deal With A Narcissist

Often times, narcissists can be difficult to avoid. In both work and personal life, there are narcissists whom you need to hang out with. You may even have the feeling that your partner is a narcissist. Therefore it is beneficial to know how to handle them properly.

While not all traits of a narcissist need to be negative by definition, a narcissist is often difficult to deal with in the long run. In a relationship, there is often talk of psychological violence from a narcissist. If you are not mentally strong, a narcissist can do a lot of damage and you can become insecure.

Getting along with Narcissists

It's difficult with terrific narcissists. Your devaluations, outbursts of anger, showing off make the counterpart to create.They are unbearable as a relationship partner, difficult to handle as a supervisor or colleague. The following tips can help: Make yourself aware that behind the arrogant facade there is a humiliated person. Don't take his behavior personally. You can also do an imagination exercise for this purpose: Imagine that you are sitting in a pyramid in which you are 100 percent protected. On the outside it is decorated with lots of mirrors. Any attacker who approaches them only gets their own behavior reflected back. Prepare a few response strategies. It is important that you show your limits in a calm way. The answers don't have to be particularly witty. If a narcissistic boss yells at you repeatedly, each time you can say:"No information would have been lost if you had said this kindly." If you feel overwhelmed in the face of Wutattacke can "Down silence" be a strategy. You look at the narcissist in silence until he's back down.

Narcissists need praise like air. Praise the narcissist for doing something well. However, the praise should be meant seriously.

Give up all expectations that the narcissist will recognize you as you would like. Keep repeating to yourself: He cannot communicate on an equal footing, and the problem is NOT yours. Strengthen your self-worth when dealing with empathetic people and activities that you build.

Think about your own shares. Unless you are dealing with the narcissist through external compulsions, ask yourself why you are spending time with the narcissist. Are you chasing his approval in vain? What old patterns of yours does he use? Or are you too unwilling to dare to try new things by holding onto a relationship or a job? Take the encounter as a sporting challenge, to practice calmness or to change something in your life.

- **Try to pack criticism well**

Since narcissists are not particularly capable of criticism, it is important to prepare well in advance for the expression of criticism. This is mostly the case when the person concerned is an authority figure. In general, you should start your criticism with praise. It is best to direct your focus on the appreciative part and present the mistakes as an oversight. If your counterpart still reacts violently to the criticism, it is advisable to accept the reaction and not refer to yourself. Often such a reaction is only a protective function of the cracked self-esteem.

- **Set boundaries**

In an interpersonal relationship with a narcissist, you should be stuck with boundaries from the start. A narcissist tends to take advantage of other people and make them bad, so you should pull the emergency brake early on. If the self-satisfied behavior goes too far for you, you should make it clear to your counterpart gently in order to protect yourself.

- **See the positive qualities**

Narcissism has benefits too. While narcissists can often be difficult to work with and deal with, there are also many qualities that are positive. Narcissists are not shy about approaching others openly and are interested in the lives of others. In addition, they are usually very humorous and entertaining and can attract attention due to their interesting nature. In addition, they are open about their opinions and have good assertiveness. You can lead by example and encourage others to believe in yourself and your abilities. This is why narcissism works particularly well in the executive suite.

How to work with a narcissist

Although a narcissist will always be dominant, it is relatively easy to get something from them. One shouldn't expect to be able to talk about collaboration, but one can work with a narcissist if one applies some basic principles.

- **Praise**

When you praise a narcissist's achievement, you create an opening to add some of your ideas. Then if you make him feel like it was his idea, or at least was inspired by his brilliant ideas, he'll soon be inclined to come with you. In fact, it may even happen that through this behavior he will idealize you, and then you will achieve a lot with a narcissist.

- **Avoid any form of criticism**

If you consciously or unconsciously criticize a narcissist, they will never forgive you. Take the blame on yourself before the narcissist can blame you and compliment them on what they did well.

- **Let the narcissist be great**

Please do everything possible to confirm the narcissist's self-image. Let him be great. For example, by making yourself or your contribution small and insignificant.

- **Be silent about the nonsense a narcissist tells you.**

Whatever lie or nonsense the narcissist tells, don't argue with him. Be quiet or agree with what has been said, but do not engage in a confrontation. You won't lose a discussion if you're right, but you won't win it either. It is a shame to try and you will get nothing more from the narcissist.

- **Make sure that you remain valuable**

Since a narcissist only thinks in his / her profit, he will end the cooperation when you have no more value. From "hero" to "zero", with a narcissist it happens in a second. Remember that a narcissist will only want to do something to you if he or she benefits from it.

CHAPTER SIX

Setting Boundaries and Interacting With a Covert Narcissist

One of the key things you need to do to take back control from the narcissist is to set boundaries. Setting boundaries with a toxic person canhelp you ensure that you deflect any disrespectful communication and also help you avoid exploitative behavior from the narc.

Boundaries are essentially a measure of your self-esteem. They are a way of setting limits for the behaviors you're willing to accept. Once you successfully implement boundaries (which takes effort on your part to ensure you are consistent with your boundary setting), you're taking back control. You are determining whether or not someone else can make you feel put down or devalued, and you can use boundaries to stop the narc in their tracks from taking advantage of your kind heartedness.

At the moment, it's likely you have some weak boundaries in place. Weak boundaries open you up to being disrespected, emotionally damaged and mentally hurt, and a narcissist can spot weak boundaries a mile off, so it's probable that these frail boundaries are being used to the narcissist's advantage.

Replacing the boundaries you already have with stronger, more robust ones does take a little time and effort. It's all well and good to say 'no' to an unreasonable request one day, but the key to successful boundary setting is to ensure you say 'no' every time an unreasonable demand comes your way.

You need to take some time to reset your boundaries. Take some time aside to write down the specific words, phrases, actions (or lack of actions) and situations that make you feel hurt, unhappy and devalued. When you're writing these things down, it can also be quite beneficial to consider what the narcissists motivation behind these words are actions are. This can go some way into helping motivate you to stick to the boundaries you're going to set in place. This little exercise will also help you identify the weaknesses of your current boundaries.

The first boundary to be recomended is knowing where to draw the line. Which behaviors are you willing to accept, which ones aren't you? Indeed, It's one thing to say you're not going to accept a particular behavior anymore, but it's quite another to go ahead and prevent that from happening. Figuring out where you're going to draw the line is the easy part, the hard part is actually drawing the line.

You must remind yourself that your boundaries are not up for discussion or debatable. Keep in mind why you are setting these boundaries in the first place: to make you feel less overwhelmed, calmer and more in control. You're doing this for your emotional health.

If, whilst you're setting boundaries, you feel the atmosphere has become too unhealthy or toxic, it's wise to have an exit plan up your sleeve. You have the right to leave at any time; you don't need permission. However, I understand this can be hard to initiate, especially if the narcissist is being abusive, but this should make it all the more necessary for you to leave.

Your exit plan can be as simple as saying you need to leave the room to make a call or you're late for something - it doesn't matter. If needs be, you might want to message a friend to ask them to call you, so you can take yourself out of the toxic situation. If this isn't possible, you can look at your phone and say, 'I need to answer this', which will also serve to take you away from the unpleasant situation.

You don't need to give any more detail than this; it doesn't matter who's calling you, what you're late for or where else you need to be. This is of no concern to the narcissist, so don't feel like you have to offer up any reasoning with the narc. Wherever you're going or whatever you're late for, the destination is self-care, and this is something the narcissist won't comprehend, so why try to reason with them?

A great tactic to utilize when setting boundaries is to use one of the narcissists greatest assets against them: conversation manipulation. It's not as complex as it sounds, nor is there any underlying malice as there is with a narcissist doing this. this is simply steering an uncomfortable or unpleasant conversation into a different direction. The direction you'll be steering this is the narcissists greatest topic: themselves.

For example, should you be asked a question that leaves you feeling uncomfortable, you're not required to stay on the topic. Although, it's likely that you would feel backed into a corner, you can be in control of how you retort to any narcissistic jibing. For instance, if the narcissist questions what you're doing with your money, you don't need to directly answer that question. Chances are it will only lead to you being made to feel inadequate or stupid by the narcissist. Instead, shift the conversation into another direction, preferably something that bumps up the narcissist's ego. Perhaps ask them what their secret tricks are for being so good with money or how they manage to save so much money whilst making it look easy.

It may seem like this 'conversation manipulation' only serves the narcissist, and fluffs their ego, but it's a technique to ensure the focus is taken off you and placed on to the narcissist.

To further add to this, it's important to note that you don't deserve to be interrogated. It's a sad truth that the less you share with a narcissist, the less information or 'ammunition' they have to use against you. When you're being criticized, or your actions are being questioned, don't feel the need to explain or justify yourself.

For example, if the narcissist is condemning you, for whatever reason, instead of getting flustered, agitated and wanting to retort with your justifications, understand that you're simply taking their bait. Instead, you could say something like, 'thank you for your opinion, I'll certainly keep that in mind'. If they are critiquing your choices or decisions, instead of trying to get them to understand your reasoning, simply say something like 'I'm quite confident about that idea'. You can still thank them for their concern and input, but this short and to the point reply strips the narcissist of any power over the conversation. Remember that you don't deserve to be interrogated.

Another awesome way to set boundaries is to call out the narcissistic behavior that is being exhibited. It's not wise to outright name-call and accuse your abuser of being a narcissist or evil (even if this is the truth), as this will just cause an unpleasant atmosphere. On top of that, it will likely give the narcissist some ammunition to use against you; they may say you're mean, nasty, hurtful or a bully. This can then be used against you in a smear campaign, or to start an argument at a later date. Don't stoop to the narcissists level. You can be matter of fact, straight to the point and honest without being aggressive or accusatory.

As you're probably all too aware narcissists do tend to push the limits of relationships. They like to test to see what they can get away with and go that one step further to make sure they feel one up on you or others around them. When you straight up call out the behavior of a narcissist, in a non- confrontational way, the aim is to defuse their limit pushing.

For example, if the narcissist says something negative about you or depreciates an idea you may have, instead of biting, you can say something like: 'that comment sounded like you were putting me down', or 'that comment was quite hurtful. Did you mean to put me down?' Tailor your reply to match the interaction.

Don't feel the need to offer up anything else after you've called out their behavior or get into a lengthy conversation about it. Keep setting placeholders like this during negative interactions with the narcissist, and don't be drawn in if their response isn't as reasonable as you'd like. Setting boundaries takes time, as does reaping the rewards from them.

Attention is one of the narcissists biggest desires; even with a covert narcissist, who can appear meek and introverted, you ought to be under no illusion that the craving for attention is still there. Whatever they believe, say, or need is their main priority in that moment, and they do expect it to be your priority as well. This hunger for attention is ultimately draining, and to stop yourself being sucked into their narcissistic, ego-inflating needs, make sure that you're checking in with yourself.

Mentally return your focus to yourself. What do you want? What do you need? How are you feeling? Take the time to ask yourself these important questions. Though, this can be hard to do in the middle of an interaction with a narcissist, but you can still do this retrospectively after the event. This may be helpful in identifying your thoughts about the situation, and perhaps help you think about how you would like to handle the situation differently in the future. It's a great way to identify boundaries you wish to set as well.

By doing this often, you're increasing your self-awareness, and allowing yourself to become more aware of how the narcissists behavior affects you. The more you do this, the more self-awareness you have, and over time this will lessen the power the narcissist has over you. With a more assured self-awareness, the narcissists agenda will no longer overwhelm you.

This is a good place to describe the term 'grey rock'. This term is a way to approach dissociation, temporarily, when you're in an emotionally vulnerable situation. It means dialing down how much you allow yourself to care about the narcissist. You temporarily make yourself as impenetrable as a rock, disassociating yourself emotionally, and protecting yourself from unsafe situations.

Essentially this technique is allowing you to take a step back, and not feel like you have to fend off any unwanted aggression or goading from the narcissist. You're not emotionally invested, and therefore their words can't penetrate you. Allow your replies and responses to be mundane and dull, almost making yourself part of the scenery.

This technique can help you remind yourself that you need to reserve some energy for yourself, as well as for people who truly care about you. By not fully engaging with the narcissist, you're reserving that precious energy for more meaningful things. Grey rock also stops you from showing as much vulnerability and offering up as much emotion, which are things a narcissist usually clings onto. The grey rock technique decreases the likelihood that they will be able to do this, helping diminish the put downs and critiques that they would usually offer up in a situation.

Covert narcissists relish in getting a reaction out of other people. It's their perverse way of reassuring themselves that they are important, their presence matters, and they have the ability to 'get to' people. If you do bite or show emotion when they provoke you, although unintentionally, you're reinforcing then negative and unhealthy behavior. You're giving them the reaction they need.

Narcissists are adept at getting a rise out of others, so I understand that sometimes you will react, despite you knowing that it's probably better not to. But, where possible, try to set that emotional reaction to one side until later, Manipulate the conversation to revert it back to them and excuse yourself when possible. Once you're out of that unpleasant and unhealthy environment, you can go ahead and process how you feel in a much safer way. This way, you won't offer up any emotional vulnerability to the narcissist. And that leaves you a winner in this fight for power that the narcissist is insistent on winning.

It's much easier to read about the idea of setting boundaries and to think about the boundaries you want to set than it is to actually put them into action. Setting boundaries isn't just a one-time thing: it's something that you have to consciously continue to put in place. In order to help you best implement these in a way that will ensure you don't slip or give in; self-compassion is a good thing to develop.

Compassion for ourselves is something that our narcissistic partners don't encourage. In fact, in most cases, it's something they strongly discourage, in their covert, patronizing way. If you try to implement a boundary and it's not gone as successfully as you'd hoped, or if you've been too emotional or if you've allowed yourself to be manipulated yet again, give yourself some compassion. Understand that you are only human, ask yourself what you want to do differently next time and move on. Never beat yourself up about mistakes or mishaps. We need to be our own champion and give ourselves a vote of confidence.

If you find that you're overwhelmed by the way the covert narcissist makes you feel, remember that you don't need to be that person who says yes to every demand or meets there every desire. You can choose if you actually want to be around them, you can choose whether or not you want to be their source of narcissistic supply.

Whilst covert narcissists can be mean, spiteful, patronizing and can stealthily intimidate people, remember that they do feel inferior and empty on the inside. This to make you feel pity for the narcissist, but rather so that you can see them more realistically. If you think about it, it must be quite difficult to be constantly needing that narcissistic supply and craving validation from others all the time. Keep in mind their limitations to help you not take their behavior personally.

It is important to note that good, solid boundaries can also include consequences, and you need to follow through with these consequences. This doesn't mean you need to be fearful but rather use this knowledge to understand what you are prepared to do if your boundaries are violated. As an example, if you're insulted by the narcissist when you are implementing a boundary, you should have an idea of the consequence of what will happen in your mind before the situation happens - you don't want to have to figure it out in the heat of the moment. It is advisable to only communicate your desired consequence one time before carrying it out. No explanation is necessary. Once the consequence has been communicated, and this has been ignored and your boundary violated, you must take action - straight away, every single time. If you don't do this it's never going to be as effective as if you are consistent. Inconsistent boundary setting means you lose credibility and remain in the Cat and Mouse game of the narcissist.

It's also important to know that whenever you set healthy boundaries, the narcissist may up the ante on their threats, verbal attacks and gossip spreading. This is one of the sad risks of having a narcissist in your life; being with a narcissist does come at a price. You can attempt a healthy relationship with a narcissist, but you'll always be having to pick your battles and interact with your narcissist in a more mindful way than you would if you were in a non-toxic relationship.

CHAPTER SEVEN

Defend Yourself Against Slanders and Lies

The relationship with a narcissist presents a great interpersonal challenge: his excessive self-centeredness and lack of empathy towards other people make a relationship with him so difficult and uncomfortable. His inability to be empathetic, understanding and willing to compromise on others can make dealing with him hell. It is therefore very crucial to seek ways of defending yourself against narcissist behaviours.

How can one make life easier for oneself by the side of a narcissist, avoid the permanent destructive influence and preserve freedom and the chance for self-determination?

- **Eliminate its presence**

With their presence, the narcissist creates an incredible presence that is intimidating and engaging. He can manipulate other people with just his looks. He casts them under his spell and hardly anyone dares to contradict him or to criticize him. Most of them inadvertently lapse into submission and lose their own judgment.

You can only escape this strong aura of a narcissist by not accepting his statements unconditionally, but always comparing the narcissist's views with your own convictions or other points of view. The narcissist can appear very convincing with his presentation skills, eloquence and repartee skills and win over others in no time at all. You should learn, however, not to be hastily carried away into any actions or concessions in his presence. If in doubt, give yourself sufficient time to think about it. In the absence of the narcissist, it is usually better to look at the issue from all sides, to think through a decision well and to make your own judgment.

Realize that while the narcissist likes to puff himself up into a god-like figure, he is really just a person with flaws and weaknesses. You should be careful not to freeze in awe and let yourself be rendered numb as if under hypnosis. The attraction of a narcissist and his attractive charisma can be broken if you center yourself strongly, always look at his ideas and views critically and always remain aware of your own goals and needs. This is how you can preserve your autonomy.

• **Recognize his problem**

Unless you know you are dealing with a narcissist, you cannot adjust to them either. Otherwise you will think for a disproportionately long time about the reckless and egocentric behavior of the narcissist and still not come to any knowledge or goal-oriented solution. Only when you have understood narcissism can you also perceive the laws behind the narcissist's actions and try to find a way to adjust to him. On the one hand, this makes you more tolerant of his behavior and, on the other hand, he becomes more predictable for you.

The ability to understand the causes of narcissistic personality disorder is a tremendous help in understanding the narcissist's dilemma, because suddenly you no longer see a strong and unassailable person, but a small, helpless child begging for attention and cannot control his emotions. This will take away the fear and horror of this person and you will gradually even develop compassion for him, because you have understood that because of a lack of love he must continually beg for approval and confirmation in order to survive emotionally.

• Praise and heed him - but in proportion

If you don't give a narcissist what he needs most, then you will never be able to endure him. Give the narcissist sufficient praise and consideration, but do not overdo it because, on the one hand, he would not take you seriously and, on the other, you would no longer have time for yourself.

If you ignore his need for attention and admiration, if you arrogantly ignore his wishes, suggestions or concerns, and if you always know better, then you will only provoke arguments. The narcissist wants to be noticed and seeks your approval. If you deny him that, you will not be able to reach him and he will not listen to you either. You have to give him his food!

If you take your point of view too aggressively and try to persistently persuade the narcissist to change their point of view, to change his mind or to teach him, then this is not going to please him very much. Therefore, you should not express your own opinion and your true thoughts too openly, but acquire a certain diplomatic skill, on the one hand not to anger the narcissist and on the other hand not to completely deny your own convictions.

• Keep in touch with other people

You will never be number one for a narcissist - he has already reserved that place in his heart for himself. A narcissist needs freedom, variety and challenge. Since you become too ordinary for him over time, he will break out of everyday life again and again to experience new adventures. Therefore, you should know that your need for closeness cannot be satisfied by the narcissist alone.

In order not to become lonely in a relationship with a narcissist, you should maintain regular contact with other people. You can get from good friends or relatives what the narcissist denies you: sincere sympathy, trust, genuine listening, understanding, tolerance, warmth and the feeling of feeling accepted and lovable. These needs are very important for your self-esteem and need to be met.

In addition, a narcissist tends to isolate his partner from the outside world and socially isolate him. It usually begins with the fact that he talks badly about your friends and wants to forbid you to interact with them or only accepts him disapprovingly. If, however, against your better knowledge - out of a guilty conscience - you bow to his wish, you are also blocking the opportunity to exchange ideas with others, to experience other points of view than those of the narcissist and to be able to form a comprehensive opinion for yourself. You need objective and fair reflection from other people. If you only get to hear the narcissist's opinion, you will no longer be able to make a comprehensive judgment and begin to gradually give up your own beliefs.

- **Don't do therapy**

It would be unwise to attribute a personality disorder to the narcissist. Some believe that once they have recognized narcissism, they have found the problems for the relationship crisis and have to joyfully share their newfound knowledge with the narcissist. They are subject to the mistake of motivating the narcissist to a suitable therapy or possibly being able to treat him himself by informing him about his feelings of inferiority and his need for love.

But a narcissist does not see anything abnormal in their behavior. On the contrary: He considers himself to be the measure of all things and cannot find anything abnormal in his appearance, let alone come to the conclusion that he is in need of treatment. If you now play the therapist and want to explain the reasons for his inappropriate behavior, you will not enjoy your new calling for long. The narcissist will twist the word in your mouth and get you so confused that afterwards you will no longer be able to distinguish black from white.

In relationships, narcissists use skillful manipulative conversation practices to confuse their partner in such a way that they end up believing that they are disturbed themselves and then find themselves in psychotherapy. After his common sense has been overridden, the partner is completely insecure and doubts his own perception until he believes that he urgently needs to seek psychological treatment.

DON'T BELIEVE EVERYTHING HE SAYS

Men and women say they feel homesick not for narcissists, but for how they felt around them. The flattery acted on their brains like a euphoric drug. Why did those compliments worth a few cheesy and insincere pennies, those sensational gestures (apparently) by man / woman in love lost, had the power to make individuals who were anything but naive and gullible capitulate? Well-established, intelligent people who 'knew their stuff'?

Perhaps because self-confidence, when not well-established, constantly requires feedback from the outside world, making us easy prey for individuals unable to love. As long as the world's judgment weighs on us like a boulder, preventing us from seeing ourselves exactly as we are, with our strengths and weaknesses, we will continue to be fragile and defenseless like babies:

Fantasized trust depends on how we are treated by others and the world at large: we "trust" someone who treats us as we feel we should be treated, or how we believe we should treat a person. We trust those who meet our expectations, but then if this person invades us or hurts us, then we lose the "trust".

Basically, this kind of trust isn't really trust, because it depends on the outside. However, when we use the word "trust", that's what we have in mind. When we say "I trust you" or "I trust that person", we usually mean that that person has treated us in a way that makes us feel confident . But in most cases we have never really accepted that person, we have not seen them clearly, which means that sooner or later they will do something that will destroy our trust . By accumulating betrayals and invasions, we end up having a general distrust of others, even if we develop a mask of "trust" and "openness". Most of us live in this state of fantasized trust or global distrust.

By flattering, narcissists make us feel accepted for what we are not. We are not the most beautiful, we are not the best, we are not the best and we do not have super powers, not because we are inferior to others, but simply BECAUSE WE ARE NOT GOD. You will say "But he / she seemed so sincere when he told me I was the best!". Well, it was a representation designed to do with you exactly what they wanted at a later time, an automatic mechanism operated by everyone and therefore very dangerous: if you treat the flattery that others turn to you as absolute truth, you must also consider it any devaluations and destructive criticisms as such. The others will become the undisputed judges of your beauty or skill and then try to imagine where your trust will go!

Ordinarily, our idea of mistrust is just as unconscious as that of trust. When we feel distrust of someone it is often an emotional reaction, not a mature response. The fact is that when someone says or does something that makes us feel disheartened, they are going to touch a space within us that was already deeply hurt and disheartened. He opened our bank of distrust, so to speak, which for a long time continued to receive and accumulate deposits.

We call this kind of distrust "global distrust" because it has no discernment, objectivity or clarity. It is an emotionally tainted state of our past history of betrayal and invasion, which strongly colors the way we experience the present. When we are provoked, unconscious memories awaken in us of when in the past, especially as children, we were invaded or betrayed.

At that time our mistrust was formed, starting from the traumas we suffered, which gradually froze. It hides in the basement of our conscience, waiting for the provocations we encounter in our daily life. These provocations can come to us from lovers, friends, authority figures, children or parents - in short, from someone who we have invested our energy in, from anyone who is in any way important to us.We can also be triggered by simple life events. And when our distrust is provoked we feel not only the present betrayal, but also all those past betrayals that we have accumulated. Distrust can be so strong that it sabotages relationships and work situations. We want to stick to our fantasies, and each new betrayal simply adds to the already long list of deceptions.

When a narcissist promises you something and then doesn't do it, when they pretend to have forgotten about the program, the trip, the dinner, your wedding anniversary, your birthday, a child's birthday, when they leave for a sudden trip without giving you (on purpose) time to organize yourself to accompany him / her, how did you feel? Usually there is a sort of regression to a childhood state where our dad, for example, promised to take us to the park by bicycle but then decided to stay home and read the newspaper, causing our anger and disappointment.

To trust is to give energy. We know that energy vampires absolutely need your life energy to find the strength and vigor that allows them to act absolutely undisturbed when they harm you. Your trust is essential for maintaining serenity in the pseudo relationship in which you have been or still remain entangled. If you have the slightest suspicion that while they say they love you they are doing the opposite, if you sense that destroying your self-esteem and psychically killing yourself is part of a strategy to keep yourself in control for life, it is obvious that the only option left is to blow the wheels. of the wagon to leave on foot and run as soon as possible. No human being in the world tolerates for long the burden of suffering that involves living in doubt and suspicion ... unless these doubts and suspicions are replaced by a new injection of blind and reckless trust in the relationship that starts from one alone, that is, right from you. Here, by denying you the right to make the best choice to protect yourself from future ills, perverse narcissists deny you the power and control over your life. Only he / she can decide when and whether to leave the relationship. The power and control over you must be absolute otherwise, as you well know, the teasing and devaluations increase dramatically because "you do not trust him / her". This is why it is important, even when caught 'red handed', to continue begging for your undisputed and absolute trust, while firing the volleys of lies you know well. When a perverse narcissist realizes that you trust him again, what happens inside him? He feels omnipotent, just like you feel or felt when he flattered you. The mechanism could be summed up like this: the narcissist flatters you - you trust him - he feels powerful because he keeps you at bay and therefore is free to do whatever he wants.

By keeping you 'good' and convincing you of their infinite love, they manage to juggle in the most difficult situations without arousing any suspicion. It is an exchange relationship in which their flattery is amply rewarded by your unconditional trust, a real fuel for them, it would seem very exciting because they see you as poor naive and gullible, devoid of intelligence because belonging to an inferior humanity. which must be exploited and squeezed like a lemon by "higher beings" like them.

There is no limit to their lies

Sometimes narcissists will play the extreme mercy card by telling you that they have a mental health problem and that you are therefore a bad person because you don't understand them.

"They might claim that they have a substance abuse problem because they're depressed or because they're anxious, " Neo said. "My ex came up with a diagnosis of 'borderline personality disorder': people with this serious illness are emotionally unstable because they can't regulate their emotions.

For this he took the opportunity to say that he was paranoid and therefore he did not like me talking to other people ".

Over time, narcissists become more and more adept as they learn how to manipulate people on a daily basis. Basically, the only significant thing you can do is to get as far away from them as possible. You should leave as soon as you realize you are living with a narcissist.

The best form revenge you can achieve is to live your life, learn from experience, and grow accordingly. Finding out that they are stronger and happier without them drives them crazy.

DON'T EXPECT HIM TO BE ABLE TO ASSUME HIS RESPONSIBILITY

Narcissists fail to put themselves in the shoes of the people around them. This is especially evident on an emotional level, due to a reality that does not go unnoticed: they do not apologize for the damage, the wrongs done or the mistakes committed.

The narcissist from afar may seem charming, confident, and focused on their goals. However, especially in the relationship of a couple, he is unable to apologize , assume his responsibilities, run for cover. Experts argue that this is due to a self-centered and dominant disposition, where there is no trace of empathy.

Disagreements and conflicts are frequent in our relationships of friendship, couple, work and family . Furthermore, often and almost without being aware of it, we can offend or even hurt others. In these cases, we do not hesitate to sincerely apologize to repair the damage and to learn from what happened. The goal is to ensure it doesn't happen again.

The greater the social and emotional intelligence, the greater will be the predisposition not only to apologize , but also to do so effectively. In these cases, the person skilled at managing these skills employs a certain emotional openness, great sincerity and a desire to remedy what has happened.

What happens in the case of narcissists? Education such as the one conducted by Joos M. Leunissen and Constantine Sedikides, of the University of Nottingham, tell us clearly: this profile does not always feel a sense of guilt for the transgressions committed.

Although he feels socially pressured to have to remedy the situation, it causes him to struggle, resist, and even suffer from making his own ego vulnerable. Let's see more data on this.

The narcissistic personality presents itself at different stages. This profile goes, in fact, from a normal state (where there is a more or less adequate regulation of self - esteem) to that pathological extreme that defines the narcissistic personality disorder.

In the latter case, the subject needs to build and protect the image of a clearly abnormal ego . Thanks to this, he manages to protect that particularly weak and fragmented inner part: self-esteem. He aspires, therefore, to give an image of himself as a profoundly efficient, perfect and omnipotent person.

So what happens when the narcissist commits a transgression? What happens when he is accused of disrespect, of being offensive, selfish or inattentive? He can't take this blame. Doing so causes a conflict with the image of perfection that it strives to maintain.

The narcissist will make you believe the mistake is yours

We know that apologizing is generally a step the narcissist will not take. Now, an even more complex and contradictory action could occur.

This personality, hard as it is to believe, suffers a lot. He suffers intensely because he always feels frustrated and bitter. His low self-esteem puts him on the battlefield, where he must stand out with his shiniest armor and largest crown.

This need to flaunt perfection, efficiency and be haughty very often clashes with a reality that does not tolerate this type of attitude.

A situation that occurs very often in a relationship is that when the partner demands an apology for a concrete situation, the narcissist will make him believe that the fault is his . The reason? He doesn't understand, he doesn't see things like others, he is weak or even ignorant.

Almost without realizing it, he can change the cards on the table. Let's not forget, in fact, that people with narcissistic disorder are skilled manipulators , so it is very likely that the injured party will apologize.

DON'T ASSUME THAT HE CAN SHARE THE SAME VALUES AS YOU

Anyone who nevertheless attracts the wrong side of a narcissist should try to keep calm. He should not forget that it is actually the narcissist's personal feelings of inferiority that cause him to scream and get angry. It is very vital that you do not provide the narcissist with any insight into your private life or share emotions or feelings with him.

You should always ensure you remain highly professional and not keep any non-professional relationships or contact with a narcissist. You can only secure or protect yourself if you give the narcissist as little attack surface as possible. This is simply because the day will come when he will ruthlessly exploit this knowledge to his advantage. Narcissists are usually treatable in the rarest of cases because experience has shown that a narcissist would never get the idea that he might be in need of therapy.

Trying to be a narcissist's savior can quickly lead to a situation where you need therapy yourself. Ultimately, you would likely have to sit out narcissists. At some critical point they too are known make a crucial mistake because in all seven versions of the story about the selfish youth it always comes down to the same thing: "Narkissos always crashes". Which solves the problem by itself.

DON'T EXPECT HIM TO CHANGE

Thinking you can change a narcissist is like a game of slaughter. He just wants his partner to accommodate all of his wishes. Always on the defensive, in fear of giving her too much power, he is impatient and touchy. He can't stand being criticized and reacts in an angry way even for a trivial note she makes to him.

The relationship with a manipulative narcissist is characterized by being a relationship of dependence and manipulation, which follows the slave-master or victim executioner dynamic. The master / executioner considers his prey as an object, a means to confirm his superiority while the slave / victim is gradually impoverished of every resource to please the executioner more and more. Paradoxically, in this scheme the figure of the victim / slave has an advantage, that of having the ability to set himself free from the chains of a manipulative relationship.

The only way out is to change and not expect the narcissist to change or understand, he considers the victim only as a tool in his hands to satisfy his needs and above all he does not suffer from the consequences of his actions. The victim of a manipulative narcissist has not been able to protect himself and identify the danger.

Whatever you answer will never go well, for a manipulative narcissist there is never the right answer, for him you will always say the wrong thing because you don't understand. so the first step is to give up the desire to save one's executioner and to want to modify it to make it resemble one's ideal of man. Facing a manipulator is not easy because he is a true expert on the subject, he will make you feel guilty, will leverage your feelings or will attack you by humiliating you, instilling in you the doubt that you have done something wrong, to make you retrace your steps and get closer to him.

To eliminate the dependent relationship with a manipulative narcissist, it is essential:

- not to start arguing with him / her since any discussion will turn into a fight or blackmail, communication is always impregnated with manipulation, so behind his words there is it is always the need to subject to its need.

- evaluate only the actions and not the words, since the latter uses them with skill in order to create an imaginary reality aimed at ensnaring you but soon his usual negative behaviors will bring you back to earth.

- be wary of anything that forces you to do or requires you, the manipulative narcissist is able to create in you the idea that being in a couple implies pleasing him and following his every request. When this does not happen it makes you feel wrong and gives you guilt.

- accept the idea that you can never be a perfect partner, everyone has their weaknesses but this does not mean not being lovable or not knowing how to love. A manipulative narcissist will always judge you and you will never feel up to it.

- communication must be simple, clear and non-aggressive, a question is followed by a precise answer, avoid direct criticism that is nothing more than a bait that he will bite by creating endless discussions. The manipulative narcissist does not establish a dialogue but only makes a monologue.

- the relationship with a manipulative narcissist is characterized by the hyper-adaptation of one's partner to him, this means that the victim never has time for himself but must devote himself exclusively to him. Start carving out time for yourself without justifying your choices, decide and behave accordingly.

- do not react to provocations

- seek economic independence if there is none

- rebuild a network of friendships and contacts from which the perverted narcissist distances his own victims. Relationships are a valid support in the moments in which the executioner attacks the victim and empties her of all capacity and self-awareness. decide and act accordingly

- do not react to provocations
- seek economic independence if there is none

- rebuild a network of friendships and contacts from which the perverse narcissist distances his victims. Relationships are a valid support in the moments in which the executioner attacks the victim and empties her of all capacity and self-awareness. decide and act accordingly

- do not react to provocations

- seek economic independence if there is none

- rebuild a network of friendships and contacts from which the perverse narcissist distances his victims. Relationships are a valid support in the moments in which the executioner attacks the victim and empties her of all capacity and self-awareness.

A relationship must guarantee the autonomy of the members that compose it, each remains himself while getting closer to the other. The master / executioner and victim / slave couple, on the other hand, are characterized by a destructive interlocking, in which the former uses his partner as a resource from which to draw energy to complete himself, never allowing her to get too close. The narcissistic paradox consists in seeking the other, absorbing their energy and denying their existence at the same time. An attachment is created between the two components of the couple that destroys the victim, his desires and aspirations whenever he does not satisfy or question the manipulator's requests. The only way not to get stuck in such a relationship is to stay yourself, set limits and ask for respect.

DON'T FEED HIM WITH YOUR ANGER

If you have been in a relationship with a narcissist , you are certainly experiencing a moment of intense anger and desire for revenge between the various stages of the healing process.

Anger, however, is a parasitic and destructive feeling internalized by the victim, which slows down the healing process and - paradoxically - reinforces the addiction.

If you have a long relationship with a pathological narcissist, you have surely learned to collude with the angry and persecutory dynamic of your attacker.

In a certain sense you realize that he / she has revealed pathological aspects in you or has deposited the germ of persecution in you and you, even if you want, are no longer able to avoid reacting.

Your reaction is the aggressor's source of narcissistic nourishment.To be able to "suck", a vampire needs to see you beautiful red in the face and then attack your neck and drag you into his world.

Your reaction to a narcissist means that he / she exists and is important to you, but above all that he / she still has control over you and the relationship.

Affective dependence on a narcissist has brooding and the desire for revenge as its primary symptom.

Anger is a natural consequence of this dynamic and must be understood and accepted above all by the therapist who encounters it, but it must also be framed as a parasitic symptom, which in fact acts as a hook for the narcissist to continue to supply energy from the victim.

The proof of this is given by the fact that when the cycle of anger is interrupted, narcissists react by launching new attacks that can pass as an attempt at seduction or an accusatory-victimistic sermon.

One technique is certainly that of 'projective identification'. It is a defense mechanism, which deludes the subject of being able to control the other by inducing him to have behaviors and attitudes corresponding to his own expectations, thus denying his own feelings of powerlessness; or that progressively empties the subject of its affective and ideational contents, ending up impoverishing it. On this basis, a perverse interpersonal dynamic can be triggered, for which there is confusion about the real belonging of negative feelings ("who started first"), and the partner himself can collusively and unconsciously contribute to maintaining the misunderstanding.

If you forgive him / her without putting a boundary, in the next step he will almost certainly try to widen your window of tolerance even further.

The goal of the narcissist is to recover the relationship with the victim to re-establish the dynamics of addiction and strengthen it through mechanisms of punitive revenge.

DON'T TAKE TOO MANY STEPS BACK

Putting an end to a relationship with a known narcissist is somehow difficult, for several reasons. Your compassion, loyalty, and desire to be sincere and true to your promises make it difficult for you to consider ending the relationship. Narcissists can also make abandonment difficult because they want to be in sole control of the decision to end the relationship.

As long as the idea of maintaining the relationship at any cost is the most important thing to you, the narcissist will have the power to dominate you and manipulate your decisions.

Partners who feel the other's duty to care most strongly decide to leave only when the narcissists cross a line that they cannot or no longer want to tolerate . For a long time now, it has generally been difficult to ascertain or predict when a partner with these characteristics will abandon the boat. The patient whose narcissistic husband had suffered a stroke, even becoming physically violent did not feel it. Unlike the patient whose husband had transferred her pregnant lover into the guest room, swearing that she was an old college friend. Here, fortunately she filed for divorce.It seems that men who are injured and strongly feel this "caring" seem less likely to abandon women, perhaps due to the weight of the extra responsibility they culturally feel they have in caring for them.

When the "caretakers" finally leave they find it difficult to stick to their decision due to too much guilt or pity they feel for the ex-narcissist. If the narcissist does not want them to leave, they will continue to pressure them to change their mind ... often with the same old promises of change.

A narcissist can make your life extremely difficult in order to keep control over you through a semblance of relationship.

Will a narcissist ever be the first to leave?

Sometimes a trigger event will motivate the narcissist to abandon you. They are usually major events, which alter a person's life. If you get sick, develop a disability, if you cannot or do not want to participate in the life the narcissist has designed for you, rest assured that he may leave. Even an obviously positive event, such as the birth of a child, can upset the delicate balance of the relationship, especially if you ask the narcissist for a little more responsibility and emotional involvement. Illness, aging, job loss, or promotions that put you on a higher level than theirs can act as triggers, leading to abrupt termination of the relationship.

Irrespective of who makes the first move to leave, what you can expect at the end of a relationship with a Narcissist include:

- **The Entire Liability Will Be On You**

When things don't work out, the narcissist places the responsibility entirely on someone else. You were on the pedestal at the beginning of the relationship, as wonderful and perfect beings. The narcissist was happy to have "won" you as a life partner. Now that they see the relationship as imperfect, damaged, and over, the fault is yours alone. They may go around saying it's over because you were too fat, too needy, or that you took intercourse for granted. You have destroyed everything, broken trust, ruined the best thing you ever had: their "love" for you. You were never satisfied with the sacrifices they made for you. You will not have become what you are now without their hand. You have destroyed all that you have built together on your own. Selfish and demanding, that's what you are. In short, within 24 hours you will become the most despised person in the life of a narcissist.

Obviously it's a shocking, offensive, terrible thing, and absolutely unfair. When a narcissist gets to this point they will no longer listen to you or try to take anything you say into consideration. They may refuse to talk to you. If you apologize desperately enough and beg for reconciliation, you can get back together for a while, but things between you will never go back to the way they started.

- **Attempts To Convince That You Have Made The Biggest Mistake Of Your Life**

After months or years in which the narcissist has wronged you about everything, in which you see your every decision devalued by him / her, you will probably be inclined to doubt yourself. At that point the narcissists will surely try to convince you that you are making a colossal mistake. They will try with their charisma, persuasion, manipulation and then with intimidation, provocation and coercion to regain control of the relationship.

A narcissistic person will tell you things like, "You just misunderstood what I said. It's obvious! Basically you should know that I love you; Why did I have to say it all the time? And all the good moments we had together, didn't they mean anything to you? Just look at the negative side. You don't understand the stress I've been having lately. You take things too personally. You're exaggerating, and you know it. You are too emotional! ".

Even though narcissists try to sound positive when they try to put all the "goodness" of the relationship in your head and why you don't have to walk away, you will notice that all their "reasons" are actually negative comments about you: you are all wrong. If you think about it, they are not real encouragement to stay in the relationship but, in reality, manipulations to lower your self-esteem and make you stay.

If persuasion and manipulation don't work, a narcissist can throw up a whole range of particularly negative judgments to tread on your pain points and make you feel terrible about yourself: "You were nothing before you got married to me. Return to that stupid family of yours and rot with them. You will be a lot sorry when I am in California making a lot of money. I am so capable of finding someone who really loves me and who always puts me first . "

If the narcissist still needs to exploit you, they will never allow you to upset their plans.

Your estrangement gives you more emotional strength and power, so they cannot allow that to happen. For a control freak this is a major defeat.

- **Attempts To Give You Guilt And Recovery**

Guilt is a powerful tool used by a narcissist to suck you into the relationship. Whenever they do something nice for you, narcissists put it in the spotlight, emphasize how important you are to them, or remind you of the wonderful times you've been together. If the positive factors don't work to bring you back, they will default on you and start blatant bouts of devaluation. Any complaints you have made about their actions will be turned against you. Narcissists constantly blame their partners for the behaviors they are actually exhibiting at the moment: yelling, insults, hostility, selfishness, hatred, and passive aggression, to name a few.

Being called selfish, rude, cruel, greedy, stingy, or accused of hurting someone's feelings can be particularly painful for a person who cares about others in their heart. You have worked so hard to never be or do something bad that being accused of something you can't even feel (or rarely feel) can deeply offend you. These comments are a clear indication that the narcissist doesn't know you and doesn't see you for who you are, and this can be truly heartbreaking. This type of accusation increases your feelings of guilt, so you are more likely to increase your efforts to prove to the narcissist that you are not that type of person.

Well, that's what they want! They found a way to hang up. Once they have pushed you to react, they can make you feel helpless and guilty to the point of reversing and re-entering the relationship so that they are later to deliver the final blow.

- **Requests For Attention, Even After Breakage**

It is easier to leave a narcissist when you cut off as much contact with them as possible. However, be aware that they can be extremely persistent in grabbing your attention.

If you have children together, these requests for attention can go on and on. One patient was so anxious from all the pressure that she lost her voice when she saw her ex-husband. The man was so determined to capture her attention that he even pushed his "court" to "order" her to speak with him in public "for the sake of the children." Of course, it was really his selfish need for validation that led.

- **Promises Of Change**

If persuasion, guilt, and attention-grabbing behaviors don't bring you back to the relationship, the narcissist pulls the infamous promise of change out of the hat. Suddenly he says he understands why you are upset and says he is ready to go. It seems to you that he is fully accountable for his shocking behavior. He / she promises to go to therapy, does everything you ask for and everything your way. He claims to be very, very sorry for hurting you!

This is a tempting appeal for a person used to caring and who wants the relationship to work . It appears that the narcissist now understands what you have said and is ready to do things right. It all seems truly sincere to you! You give a sigh of relief and hope grows within you once again. Inevitably, this hope disintegrates in a short time.

- **Need**

Narcissists seem to be strong and independent, but in reality they are extremely needy. It is really difficult to stop caring for them. They might make calls asking you to go get their car fixed, they might expect you to keep doing the bookkeeping of their business, expect you to go and take out the Christmas lights at their house, or expect you to make dentist appointments for them, for example. It can be difficult and exhausting for you to say no to persistent requests of this kind.

The fact is that too often, you will find that every interaction with a narcissist involves an action on your part that only benefits him / her.

DON'T BE VINDICTIVE

Being vindictive is never a good thing, much less when dealing with a narcissist. Narcissists are extremely competitive and may see your revenge as inspiring . They may be amused by your attitude and, to keep up with you, kick out their worst side!

Instead of choosing to be vindictive, think carefully about your desired goals. Since a vengeance is never healthy, let's turn it into something constructive for yourself and for your well-being. You can get back at a narcissist by simply focusing more on yourself and neglecting all of their needs. You can achieve this by doing the following:

1. Look after your appearance

Narcissists love to be around people of good looks. Sure, you can say that everyone likes being with a beautiful woman but narcissists a little more: they want to have what everyone else wants! Your first revenge is this: take care of your appearance, improve yourself! Exercise, massage, look after your face, treat yourself to a manicure and always dress in top style.

2. Learn to be more confident in yourself

The narcissist feeds on your insecurities. By strengthening your self-esteem, you will make yourself impenetrable to its manipulative traps and, at the same time, you will appear brighter.

3. Keep your distance

Rather than being vindictive, you should end the relationship and distance yourself as much as possible. If for whatever reason you can't leave the narcissist behind (maybe he is your ex-husband and you're trying to raise a child together), then keep your distance. Don't let him invade your space and your privacy.

4. Always put yourself first

Always putting yourself first means not giving up for the narcissist, not giving up on yourself! Never put yourself in the background! Respect your life priorities. For one thing, don't give up coffee with a friend just because the narcissist would like to see you that very afternoon.

If, as assumed before, the narcissist is your ex and maybe you still have common perspectives (share the job or otherwise), putting yourself in the foreground means that in the search for compromises you really have to meet really halfway. Be careful not to give up.

5. Keep busy

By focusing more on yourself, you will have the opportunity to develop new interests or take care of pre-existing ones. Take advantage of it to keep yourself busy and lead a satisfying life: if you like swimming in the pool, invest in a membership and spend your time like this. The narcissist will hate the idea that you have other interests outside of their world.

6. Collect your satisfaction

Increase your introspective capacity, try to understand what you really want to be satisfied. Your independent and autonomous satisfaction will drive the narcissist crazy! It will be hard for the narcissist to realize that you can be satisfied even without him.

7. Awareness about personality disorder

Increase your awareness of the pathology of those in front of you. Already, many forget that narcissism is a personality disorder . In front of you is a person with several cognitive deficits . The narcissist is someone who has little chance of being truly happy. Always remember that.

8. Indifference

If he tells you about one of his titanic exploits, don't blink. You don't have to belittle what he does or what he thinks... just don't get reacted!

9. Narcissists are vulnerable

A narcissist is unlikely to admit that he has a disorder but he is not invulnerable for that. A narcissist will never go to a psychotherapeutic office shouting " I want to cure my narcissism", however he may suffer from insomnia, anxiety, may go through periods of depression, may feel agitated.... You can leverage these frailties to insinuate some doubts about the nature of his ailments. Don't forget that many narcissists are also hypochondriacs.

Some narcissists can suffer from emotional addiction .

10. The fake compliments

When it comes to a narcissist, you don't need to despise him to make him feel offended. Try giving him fake compliments. How? With nonchalance ... you give compliments like " ah, these nice shoes ... the ones you wore last time just couldn't be looked at" . Okay, you are saying that he has nice shoes but he will not focus on that, he will focus on the fact that the others were terrible and he will feel offended.

CHAPTER EIGHT

Learn To Cope With A Narcissist

It's very important to protect one's mind and emotions. With that being stated, let's find out how to cope with a narcissist. This involves making use of healthy limits with the narcissist, or in some cases, avoiding them altogether. Below are a couple of vital points:

- **Awareness**

When you are in a relationship with this person or a narcissist is a family member, you need to always pay close attention to the things they do or say. The narcissist really wants you to be unaware since this is one of their ways of maintaining control.

During this time of lack of knowledge, the narcissist can trigger all sorts of havoc in your life. This will halt numerous of the narcissist's intended actions.

- **Emotions**

Control and manage those emotions! For no reason must you let your feelings get out of control. The narcissist feeds off your lost mood, unhappiness, or elevated joy for a couple of reasons.

One reason that narcissists want you to end up being emotional is so they can call you insane or location blame on you for acting illogical. They will say words or do things that are intended to attract a remarkable reaction. You should not fall for that.

The narcissist will attempt to make you emotional so they can get attention. Any kind of attention is fine, even if they are only able to make you upset.

Disregard random insults or comments meant to activate your feelings. You will eventually be fine and the narcissist will see that they do not have control of the situation if you stick to the subject and put up your walls.

- **Self-respect**

Always stay strong in your self-regard. Among the narcissist's goals is to decrease your self-esteem. This is because their self-confidence is nearly non-existent, contrary to what they attempt to portray with lofty speech.

Destroying your self-confidence will help them feel better about themselves. It can be catastrophic in their minds if they stop working to do so. Envision being filled with absolutely nothing other than panic-- no compound and no taste.

You must maintain your self-regard and force the narcissist to either flee or take a truthful take a look at themselves. This puts an instant stop to manipulation.

- **Ego Stroking**

Okay, so this is not the best concept on earth; however it does help momentarily. You have to reframe your conversation if you have no option but to be in the business of a narcissist. Rather of asking for things for yourself, like, god forbid, regard, tell the narcissist all the benefits they will enjoy from what you desire. This is a special way to deal with a narcissist.

If you want to go to a friend's party and the narcissist is being difficult and insensitive, then ask in various ways than typical.

State this: "Everyone likes you and would enjoy your existence at the celebration."

Beware; however, this trick is only momentary and not the healthiest solution in the long run.

- **Elimination**

If all else stops working, you need to remove the narcissist from your life. If you have children with the narcissist, you might also find this impossible.

If the narcissist is simply your partner or if you do not have children together, it may be time to let go entirely. Remember, your physical and mental health is more vital than maintaining a bad relationship. Pick carefully in this area.

- **Do Not Withdraw Into Yourself But React**

Some have explained demand/withdraw as the most harmful of relationship patterns for an excellent reason: It's part of a downward spiral that frequently fails the relationship. You do not require a narcissist in the dyad, by the way, to have the pattern take over. The pattern is especially toxic because escalation is built into it-- needs unanswered, the person requiring will end up being increasingly annoyed and normally louder.

The narcissist's routine of playing hot potato implies that put in the withdraw position, he or she will either withdraw or become extremely aggressive-- blaming his or her spouse for making the demand in the first place, casting it as an indication of his or her flawed nature, etc. That's hot potato integrated with a timeless harmful pattern.

An egotistical partner has an inflated sense of self-importance. When they are told otherwise or criticized, they strike back on no end and would go to terrific extents of embarrassing you. You must comprehend their pattern of habits.

Here are tips on how to endure narcissistic abuse:

- **Do not expose your weak side.**

Narcissists lack empathy. They do not have compassion for anybody who reveals that they are emotionally vulnerable. You will constantly be an easy target for your partner if you easily show unhappiness, sorrow or anger.

- **Don't rely on your partner to change.**

Your role is not to change your partner's egotistical personality. Assume that they will always be this way and it is not up to you to save them. You will suffer much more and experience frustration, hurt and anger over and over again.

- **Create individual limits.**

Make sure you look after your own needs before anything else. They will attempt to manipulate you into doing things that you don't want to do and make you feel guilty when you resist.

- **Learn to forgive.**

People who experience narcissism do not now that they are injuring other individuals. Their mental disease prevents them from operating harmoniously with the rest people. You know better, which puts you in a much better position to understand their situation. Forgiveness enables you to recover faster as you acknowledge that you have the power to change how your own life plays out.

Exit a violent and uncondusive relationship as soon as you can. The longer you remain in one, will amount to flexibility and joy lost. Don't think twice to reach out for assistance when you need it. You will discover that people are frequently ready to help you. You are not alone in your battle. You will find that others are likewise in the exact same boat as you are. Be amongst those who will be able to start life anew.

CONCLUSION

You need to get a new picture of your relationship if you want to stay together with the narcissist. The narcissist wants you to be at your disposal when they want it. For this reason you have to be available to him at all times without criticism. If you can let yourself get into the fact that the narcissist and not your mutual love is the most important thing in the relationship and at the same time you can build a life of your own to lead in his absence, then maybe the relationship can work.

Relationship with a narcissist never has anything to do with real partnership. It is a hierarchical relationship in which the narcissist leads and acts out and the partner serves him and sacrifices himself. He will always have to forfeit a piece of his freedom. However, a smart partner who is aware of narcissism and has seen through the nature of the narcissist knows that sometimes he must serve in order to lead.

CPSIA information can be obtained
at www.ICGtesting.com
Printed in the USA
LVHW022047031220
673316LV00007B/290